THE HOAX POEMS

THE
HOAX
POEMS

LESLIE GRACE MCMURTRY

Casa Urraca Press
ABIQUIU

Set in Plantin MT Pro and Cronos Pro.
Designed and set by Alex Espinosa.

25 24 23 22 1 2 3 4 5 6 7

First edition

Paperback ISBN 978-1-7351516-9-4
Exclusive hardcover ISBN 978-1-956375-01-5

CASA URRACA PRESS

an imprint of Casa Urraca, Ltd.
PO Box 1119
Abiquiu, New Mexico 87510
casaurracaltd.com

To my family and to poets everywhere: you will get there.

TABLE OF CONTENTS

AUTHOR'S NOTE

ON MY ELEVENTH BIRTHDAY, I asked for and received as a gift a book of photographs from the annals of Ripley's Believe It or Not. I remember spending the whole day looking through the book. From at least that time, I was fascinated by "freaks of nature." Not long before that birthday, I remember seeing photographs of Egyptian mummies—the unwrapped, unmasked cadavers—that alternatively frightened me and fascinated me. Such conflicting emotions fuelled my creative processes into my twenties, when I wrote the short story "Dwarves Without Giants," an imagined biopic of Anna Swan, a Scottish-Canadian woman of extraordinary proportions (over seven feet tall), of which I gave an online reading for International Women's Day 2010 for *Her Circle Ezine*.

The Hoax Poems still have an abiding if circuitous New Mexico connection: taking a class in Physical Anthropology at the University of New Mexico in the early 2000s, I was fascinated by the skulls in the lab, like the flat-headed Incan examples of artificial cranial deformation and the two-headed calf. Never far from my mind was the Laura Gilpin poem "Two-Headed Calf," introduced to me while I was studying creative writing at UNM: inherent in it the feeling of compassion for those deemed "freaks." Poetry is meant, I believe, to invite us to acknowledge our shared humanity, so it makes a perfect arena for entering the space of the reviled or different Other and extending understanding.

Before *The Hoax Poems*, though, there was a collection about the life of entrepreneur and wax modeller Marie Grosholtz Tussaud. The counterfeit of life in death (or in the never-living, like wax) captivated me. This imitation of nature crystallized into an interest in hoaxes, from the relatively minor (poet Witter Bynner and his *Spectra* hoax in the early twentieth century) to the legendary (the *War of the Worlds* panic in 1938). The latter has actually become a subject of consistent scholarly interest as some of my academic work is now about the boundary between reality and fiction in the audio space.

The Hoax Poems were inspired by many happy hours of research in the British Library in London, particularly sifting through the works of Dr. Jan Bondeson. I still have a strong—some might say macabre—interest in "mutants" (Armand Marie Leroi's term) that always manifests on my travels to new places, such as visiting the Museums of Obstetrics and Anatomy and the L. Cattaneo Museo delle Cere Anatomiche in Bologna.

PART 1:
HOAXES

THE PANIC BROADCAST, 1938

We drive in shadow,
redwoods shelter the road
this Halloween night. Static.

Like a stab, the dial
turns toward invasion, somewhere out
beyond LA. Panic, like glass.

We stare. In the rear-
view mirrors, we see our children,
not the gas stations going by.

Petrol is the last thing
on our minds. Like ghosts, we coast, til
softly, the car comes to a halt.

The tall towers open,
spill with Martians; we can only
hold hands, sit in the car. Darkness.

We can do nothing.
Our wedding bands clink in the hush.
Wait for sunup or burning trees.

THE HITLER BABY PHOTOGRAPH

Joke in density.
The devil's in you, in me,
the baby, the photographer,
the mind of the cunning
inventor/interventioner.

Is it like finding
a sign of evil, a gargoyle
after so many years
of gargling have twisted
that sneer?

The jack-o'-lantern
a poor man's gargoyle,
Poor Mad Tom's turnip.

But here, the perplexed
mother: the future
adult, looking in
his dark mirror.
It's me!
But it isn't.
Who is it?

SONNET FOR THE CARDIFF (NY) GIANT

With apologies to Hayden Curruth

He said, come look you here at what I foun':
Someone's buried a man at Stub Newell's farm.
So we came to look, paid fifty cents, dumbfound'.
It's a giant from the Bible, whose granite arm
'S bigger than a freight car. 'E's petrified,
Don'y'see, asleep or dead.   No! False alarm.
A Jesuit done carved him up with sulphuricide
To impress the Mohawk. Din't mean no harm.
Seems it were a lie: but they'd bought it,
Kept on lookin' after falsely shown.
And Humbug Barnum, well, he sought it.
And didn't mind, when thwarted, blown.
Old Hoaxy helped Hull's revenge achieved.
Clearly, it had to be seen *not* to be believed.

CZAR PETER AND THE COAGULUM

The Czar steepled his fingers,
masking the cloud from the samovar,
the white-silver frame
in the boiled glass of his teacup.
The curiosities reflected,
like the gleaming of his avaricious eye,
like an endless winter.
Pride of his collection, the pug dog
vomited by a peasant one summer.
Pickled in Dr. Klauningen's
briny jar, it never would grace,
like a French novel, a lady's warm lap.

THE FEEJEE MERMAID—
A RANT

After Gilbert and Sullivan

You're positively quaking and the newspaper's flaking
  because you've had it at hand for so long.
You've been poring like mad over completely unclad
  Madame Feejee the Mermaid Dugong.
You've been reading the tiffin from Dr. J Griffin that the
  papers have managed with squint.
And gosh you're excited that you've been invited and she'll
  soon be more than newsprint.
Your friends have sung praises after stunning their gazes on
  the New York display of the fishes.
You're sure without fail this is going to entail something
  bona fide in'll'ctually delicious.
You've reached the glass jar and you see that so far your
  siren has failed in enchantment.
And all you make out is an ape and a trout and you're
  wondering just where your Rembrandt went.
It's the ugliest prawn you've cast your eyes on, its jaws are
  so hideously sodden;
Its sunken form sneers that you're false in your fears; you
  clamor, with all, it's a fraud! In
Fact, you've been cast out, from your sole to your snout,
For you've been derailed by the greatest fish scaled—
A trick in threefold, which is worse, 'cause it's old.
(If you'd bothered to look, oldest trick in the book,
At the advertisement moreover,
You'd feel vastly clever
And not impaled by some great guppy hook.)
The day has been long—ditto, ditto my song—and thank
  goodness they're both of them over!

MUMLER'S SPIRIT PHOTOGRAPHS

double exposure
ghosts on glass plate,
giving grief silver hope

★★★

a face, a moon
of monotone, quietly yearning
in dignity for her wedding ring

★★★

her husband's arms'
ectoplasmic sheen
yet she felt their warmth

PANORAMA, APRIL 1, 1957

Hello? Is that the BBC?
I'd like to know, please,
how I can cultivate a spaghetti tree
of my very own. Analyses
of the garden soil make me
hopeful. What? The Pyrenees
variety is best for acidity?
I've got a pen if you've got recipes.
I'm sure it's delicious, but you see,
I don't know—with cheese
and meatballs—*Plant hopefully
a sprig in tomato sauce Genovese?*

ST. GEORGE AND THE DRAGON, PAOLO UCCELLO

as seen at an exhibition at the National Gallery (London) on Fakes, Forgeries, and Hoaxes

Some enterprising child
with crayon has given us a leonine lady,
white as Styrofoam, a timeless swan.
If she had a watch, she'd be checking it.
There is no vileness of stench from the bipedal
monstrosity, fished out of the nursery
with a nosebleed. A butterfly, or a moth
lingered on its wings, an iron curled its tail.
The saint's horse is in equilibrium,
frozen with its bored mount
in a one-dimensional landscape.
They insult your intelligence.
Is it real? How much?

STANLEY CLIFFORD WEYMAN

It's true, what they say:
> it's a movie reel that comes back to you
> between the bullet and the brain.

I've had a hundred faces,
walked the flamboyant sidestep
of a man who's taken the long
overland journey to Morocco,
smoked his cigarettes in a dignified
yet affected manner.
I've smelled the almond and jasmine
of a princess whose veil is as transparent
as rose water. Confessed her champion—
> now that was real.

I got her to the President, didn't I?
From mixing with those people, I ferreted
out the authentic,
the pretenders. Had my cases
carried by porters who might have known me
if I'd tipped my hat instead of striding,
ever, ever onward.
I remember how it was before the Wars.
No Technicolor sideshow can translate
the Astor, its soft red-velvet-cake-colored
drapes and private rooms.
Pola—that was never personal.
It wasn't a question of framed certificates.
My heart—and hers—was in the right place.
The problem is keeping one step ahead,
not fouling yourself up.
In between?
Offices, uniforms in shades of blue.
Ah well,
> I guess the jig is up for real this time.

THE CASE OF THE MIRACULOUS BULLET

Dear doctor, I don't
       know what I shall do. A good
girl still, though, I've just given birth. I ain't known a
       man. Were it my wound? Help me.

Dear lady, it's true
       the bullet lodged in your core
left an ugly hole.
       Two miracles in the space
of one minnie-ball. Stay calm.

The boy's in pain, doc,
       and my ma urges you to cut.
He's swelling as I
       were swollen. So help me
God, it's the minnie.

I remember. I
       tended a soldier shot,
his scrotum torn, just
       as I heard your cry of pain.
I'll introduce you to him.

THE GREAT MOON HOAX (1835)

It is well known that the telescope magnifies
Six thousand times. Herschel, cradled by stars,
Shows objects that surpass our sense and eyes.

The moon's ascension, here we theorize,
Its rapidity—revelations from the Cape,
Six thousand times, Herschel. Cradled by stars,

The magnification reveals the lunar landscape,
Slender pyramids, monstrous amethyst glowing
In rapidity. Revelations from the Cape:

Vermilion hills of vegetation overflowing
The Vale of Triad, with its bluish unicorn,
Slender pyramids, monstrous amethyst. Glowing

Copper-colored man-bats, glossy, skyborne
Over yellow crystal. Bison. Beavers. Pure,
The Vale of Triad, with its bluish unicorn.

Science illumines: *luna* nevermore obscure.
It is well known that the telescope magnifies:
Over yellow crystal, bison, beavers. Pure.
Shows objects that surpass our sense and eyes.

A VICTORIAN CHILDHOOD

It was the fashion, briefly, in those sepia-hewn days to plant toads in flowerpots, living toads, and cover them, so serenely in a bit of earth, and bury them, uncomplainingly—their golden-streaked eyes—in the back garden. A date would be marked in ink upon the calendar, deeply detailed into the square days, and the toad expected to be alive, if sluggish and pale, by the end. Oh my, it never worked, their half-decayed forms would stink up the garden if the dogs, oblivious, had not dug them up—dead, you see—by then. Once I saw the half-intact skeleton and dreamed ever afterwards of globular eyes, patient, throbbing indentations on wrinkly mottled brown slime.

THE NEW YORK *HERALD* REPORTS (1874)

She dares not stir from where she's sitting,
    The former shrew that is my wife.
A brave show she's making of her knitting
    Though I know she's fearful for her life.
I've balled up sheaves of *Herald* stacking,
    Just as innocent as you please,
While her eye's been straying to the headlines
    Like a transferrable disease.
I've petrified the dried old dear
    With reports of rampaging fauna,
For it says here, as clear as clear,
    They've escaped and more than trauma
Suffered New York's residents. "They're dead!"
    I heard her whisper. She feigned.
I was not to know she feared at all. I said,
    "I expect it's all a fabrication, plain—
Still, you can't be too careful. Twenty-seven!"
    "What?" was her reply. She wasn't shy.
"Trampled, torn limb from limb." "By heaven!"
    So indoors she stays, and peace have I,
While bears chew flesh and apes molest,
    While phantom wolves prowl 5th Avenue,
Condors gnash and panthers make a pest
    For baby prams and their retinue.
Thank you, thank you, New York Zoo!

THE PIG-FACED LADY
OF DUBLIN (I)

Imagine her
delicately sipping
from her silver trough.
A man would have
gained a wife by
playing her a melody
on a music box,
despite his grunts.
Imagine her tears
glistening on her
pig's snout.

THE PIG-FACED LADY
OF DUBLIN (II)

There once was a hospital patron
Whose face was equated with bacon.
    It was rubbish, of course
    But the rumor gained force
And ruined the life of the matron.

THE PIG-FACED LADY
OF BLACKFRIARS

Insubstantial rumor haunts
this square, not flesh and blood,
snout and bristle.

The clergyman and his wife,
they are phantoms, or perhaps
real and startled by a strange
fancy, that had caught hold of them—
but who dreams of seeing hog-faced women?

Tannakin Slinker from the lips
of a tour guide, an actress in black velvet
and lace on an atmospheric Halloween
night, could paint a picture, believable
in its minute detail, of a woodcut
Dutch woman, of beautiful deportment,
wealth, and classical charms,
but voiceless and with a pig's head,
and pig's speech, too.

It would have kept me,
this image of an unhappy ghost,
lonely and deformed in life,
descending staircases,
except for the improving moral
at the end, making us think of
Madame Leprince de Beaumont
and roses.

THE SILENT CITY

The frost encircles like chimney smoke.
The ice a secret staircase, cut-glass makes.
He steers us, fur-clad, our master guide, baroque
Merchant of the spiritual photograph, opaque,
Like the light on Muir Glacier. As the city,
Silent, himself the mirage or vision.
The wind freezes our tears on cheeks. Pity
The fool who climbs this high for mere derision.
We've asked ourselves, who are they,
Their mysterious world engraved by icy spray,
The glacier ice at any moment to break away?
Our ancestors or our future, another race in grey?
      Uncharted wasteland my ears hear ring:
      I try, but I can't see anything.

INTERLUDE

BIDDENDEN CAKES

My Easter morning stares
at me from the hard cake
handed in charity,
like hot sweet tea, steam
dimpling the dough.
An English village, down-wrapped
in its legends, its ancient tithes.
Visitors come with cameras,
to shed their world-weariness.
They're two sisters from a medieval
dream. If legend-bound,
they knew the world of the Crusades,
the portents of comets
and King Rufus struck dead.
Their joined hip focused,
not their charitable hearts.
They hadn't a particular
name.
How do you tell when your twin's
heart stops beating?
You carry her dead limbs
and stop at the altar of your joint
funeral.

THE BALLAD OF
KASPAR HAUSER

"Here lies Kaspar Hauser, riddle of his time,
His birth was unknown, his death mysterious."

Once long ago in Nuremberg
    A pale, strange boy did come.
He lurched with tender-footed step,
    Appearing drunk or dumb.

Rushed once straight unto the law:
    He could not speak a mote,
Except "dunno," but with a pen
    "Kaspar Hauser" he wrote.

Metal sent his senses whirring;
    His hearing and his sight
Were most impressive—he could read
    The Book in pitch-black night.

A doctor took the boy to care,
    The darkness to dispel.
When he had learnt to speak again,
    The boy had this to tell:

"I lived inside a tiny cage,
    I never stepped outside.
I chewed on bread and water sipped,
    A rocking horse to ride.

"I had not seen another soul
    Except the man who fed me.
One day he thrust me out of doors
    And to this town he led me.

"'Be a rider, like my father'—
          He taught me to declare.
He gave me letters, which you have,
          And left me in the square."

One letter, dated 1812—
          His mother's, it did claim;
The other, from a caretaker—
          But the writing was the same.

Who could he be, this stranger's child?
          A thousand sought the truth—
The Prince of Baden, Baden's heir?—
          All that they lacked was proof.

When twenty-one Kaspar had aged,
          A stranger dressed in black
Said "You must die" and drew a knife—
          But failed in the attack.

Oh, why did Kaspar walk alone
          The park, uncomprehending?
The man in black returned to give
          The snow a scarlet ending.

The man in black left little trace;
          Kaspar, to home he crept.
When his death was known, they say indeed
          That Baden's Duchess wept.

A riddle of his time was he,
          A strange short life of woe.
Was he the heir of Baden's house?
          We will never know.

DVOŘÁK'S PLAIN

Dvořák's plain,
capturing that wide circle,
almost a sea of emptiness.
It is haunted.
Perhaps there was no voice
echoing faintly from soil,
no children pleading with their father
to reappear, to say goodbye
or at least explain
if it were heaven or hell.
Perhaps there was no David Lang,
a name chosen randomly
for the credulous by a hoaxer
or a storyteller.
But the prairie's haunted.

THE CERNE GIANT

Sixteen years since that summer night.
We kept in touch, at first,
with wicked postcards. A wink
in the dull-edged paper, the profile
of the Queen too blowsy with shock
at the image on the reverse:

the only naked man the Royal Mail
abides. All in keeping
with the folklore, half-believed,
half-lost in cheap pints of cider.

Growing up in the shadow of the Cerne
Abbey, the town with little enough
of industry besides its pagan emblem,
which few dredged back
through their memories.

I did. I wondered how it had escaped
the Benedictine gaze, and were the monks blind?
But in my bones, I felt his age.
Beyond memory, they used to say,
as they herded the stones and swept the white.

A sea-form horse was riding in Sussex,
too, a ghost. Hillside and stone.

He would have it a lark, a bit of fun,
an added excitement to couplings
nocturnal and out of doors.
But I knew the power and wasn't surprised.

Sixteen years; she may well believe
the Giant is her real father.

PART 2:
STRANGE, STRANGE CREATURES

IPPOLITA PALEOTTI

Next to the name of a Pope, I sign
my woman's mark. *Studiosa.*
The dusty scholars are unimportant,
but like the sole specimen, the rarest
in the collection, there is value.
I will not be dissected. I am the cat
with two bodies, joined at the navel,
a curiosity for its thought processes,
considerably miraculous. A she-cat.
Maestro Aldrovandi's dissection table
crowded by doctors and one poet,
straining at the sharpened knife,
the still-living viper with its flicking tongue,
oblivious to dying, as the elders seek
to prove Aristotle wrong.

MRS. PETRUS GONZALES

It is no worse than marrying
        a hunchback,
my sister told me
        when the King made free
to marry me to his prodigy.

His Latin, at least, was
        sonorous, though what
his first tongue could be
        on Tenerife, some wild man's
bébé, who could say?

He was gentle, grateful, humble,
        matching smooth palm
to mine on the marriage
        bed. I grew to love
the braids of his hair.

Now he puts our children
        with the faces of terriers
on his knee. Now I
        trim his eyebrows
so he can see.

JOHANNES BAPTISTA

Traveling by coach in the blackest of weather
a Genoese man, sitting, polite and refined,
concealing a burden in his doublet of leather,

concealing a bad smell of rot ill-defined.
Lazarus was his introduction, by birth.
A Genoese man. Sitting, polite, and refined,

til a bump of the wheel gave cause to unearth
the head of his brother who grew from his side,
Johannes Baptista, his introduction. From birth,

a mouth that ate nothing, an infanticide
one-legged, six-toed, two unformed hands:
The head of his brother who grew from his side—

unconvinced by the sham, I made my demands
by roughly pressing this body of lead,
one-legged, six-toed, two unformed hands,

it moaned, how horribly, less alive than 'twas dead.
Traveling by coach in the blackest of weather
I roughly pressed the body of lead
concealed by his brother in a doublet of leather.

BY THE SIGN OF
THE SWAN IN THE STRAND

Peering at the glass bottle,
its mottled surface evidence
of years of soot, as a mask,
as a mirror, to ages, to stages
of dissimulation, you could scarce
believe that the old woman,
from the masses of her dull grey
hair, had sprouted a horn,
like the tendriling vine of a pumpkin.
It was consequence, she said,
of youth's folly, wearing a tight
round hat close to the forehead.
The ripeness was an egg-sized wen,
soreness of a racking headache,
then the *corne*, spiralling
somewhat west of a unicorn.
It ached like a sea dog's bones
during a storm.
                   This one in the bottle,
her second pair, on a gnarled
length of nine inches, and so hard
to hide under a plain linen cap.
One winter's morning she slipped
in the soggy street, yielding
the prodigious horn, never mind
the cracked and winded woman.

BARBARA URSLEIN

This is a tribute to my mother,
    a "true woman,"
        inviolate.

She could play the harpsichord,
    its tunes haunt
        my poor memories.

Her long hair grew
    in curly tufts
        from her ears.

Her eyes, winking Vermeer blue,
    from soft strands
        of golden tresses.

Her beard, more luxuriant
    than my father's,
        softer than a birdling's down.

My granddam I never knew,
    grown fat on gold
        after she had sold my mother.

My father's marriage was
    a poison, a license
        to exhibit her.

There is nothing worse than
    to see that hair
        iridescent with tears.

She was a "true woman,"
    not an ape, not a dog,
        but prey.

IN THE HOUSEHOLD OF CHARLES WHITE

As a lower servant, she had only
heard it rumoured. A macabre
birthday present, for someone
who spent her half-Sundays at her mother's,
an exhausting walk across Manchester,
even in the best weather, coal fire
in her lungs.
Once she left the scullery, made beds
with a wizened hand, rendered partially
useless by scalds and burns,
exchanging that for nightstands
and the cleaning of wax,
that was the first birthday she peeked
into the drawing room, to see the cabinet,
the cabinet they were forbidden to clean.
Standing before it once, face reflected
in the burnished dark oak surface,
she had been suffused with chemical
smells, something nasty, like drowned
puppies.
Her birthday she shared
with the long-dead former mistress of the house.
Long-dead, but not gone, not from this
drawing room.
The executors of the will, so she was told,
these men came to the house,
and stood, and sat, and asked
all others except the housekeeper away,
shining a magnificent light
on the gloom.

The housemaid peeked. It was
her birthday. She risked dismissal.
It was the old woman's birthday.
The cabinet came open with a wheeze,
and the chemical smell dampened
even the lungs of the executors,
who brought handkerchiefs to their brows.
Wheeled out of the cabinet
was a glass case. Inside
was the dead mistress.
It was her birthday.
They checked for pulse, for breath
frosting the glass. Her skin
was sullen, her clothes looked
diaphanous. She seemed
to move in the shivering light,
but the executors shrugged.
The terms of the will satisfied,
they closed up the cabinet again,
until next year.

CRACHAMI REMEMBERS

He's a man broken, they whisper.
He was a vagabond
with a hackneyed, musical
command of English
now crying, singing
a sad ditty of "Carolina, Carolina."

He remembers having kissed
the tiny, veiny webs of her hands,
palms the size of a thimble.
"Fairy," he mutters, turning
that inadequate word
through the gold and brown
of the Sicilian coast.

She loved the glitter of a pasteboard
tiara, or the bell of a trumpet,
or a ring on the King of England's
knuckle. It made no
difference. Her thin voice,
her thin waist.

He prayed so often, in his dreams
she was St. Lucia and the Virgin
as a girl. He hoped to kiss
her goodbye. A little queen,
in her bed of state. Who
pictured Carolina
an invalid, a freak?

She loved a frangipani biscuit
soaked in weak wine. Her baby's
tooth. Twenty inches tall.
Succumbing to a cough,
indistinguishable from the next consumptive.
Did someone hold her in her last moments?

Her father's eyes are a glass glistening,
echoed by a shy journalist.
Loved her from afar, just
as her papa had to in the end.
Enthralled.
"She spoke beautifully."

Could not beat them to the slab.
That soft skin, still as the milk
of her mother, revealing red and purple.
He could melt into the floor.
He just wants her bird bones
for a Catholic burial.

The years boil away like the flesh.
Her ocular bones open
an emptiness like a giant.

MUNITO THE MAGNIFICENT

Andiamo, wonderful dog, what do
you smell with your nose so fine?

You speak with your eyes, volatile
canine!
Your master's fingers

don't let them cheat your senses!
A bone, my fine Munito, my
kingdom for a bone!

You will beat me at dominoes!
Let us practice!
This Green Park

is for me to stretch my legs.
And so you do not grow corpulent!
Castelli! His alphabet, figures,
and learned hound.

Trust we meet with no cats,
or bitches, Munito!

It is impossible to ignore the harangue.
It is an Italian so fugged,
so thick like smoke
it scarcely registers as language.

It must be the clever dog,
the poodle in the daily show.
And this the master, in his faded
vestment, crude.
Sure, it is the man who saved
the wretch from drowning.
A woman in white
in a pool,
a would-be suicide.

It's hard to credit
just as the dog's wagging tail
challenges, as if to say:

guess the secret if you can,
for I am twice as smart
as you think I am.

SUITE ON CHUNEE

ZOO IN THE EXETER 'CHANGE

Never mind the pianoforte,
       which they roped up with twine.
Never mind the lion cubs
       that they got drunk with wine.
Never mind the bars of the cages,
       how they pained 'em,
For if they got loud,
       The Keepers, they just brained 'em.

Hey ho, but I want to know
       how they got the elephant up the stairs?

AUTOBIOGRAPHY OF CHUNEE

i.
I was a child.
On-stage nerves,
those faces were a sea,
an unimaginable optical illusion.
I grew weak at the knees,
unable to perform,
wishing I could trumpet in terror.
The candle-fat seared my trunk.

ii.
I held props between tooth and tusk
to this actor, visiting
my hay mattress.
The smells of brothers fanged
is both familiar and tinged with regret.
The actor (I have no word

for names) strays
from the welcoming of my trunk.
I flap my ears in surprise.

iii.
Nero, you could never understand.
It's like a graveyard, this music.
It reverberates through the hollows
of my elephantine skull.
It's soothing and yet speaks of mortality,
the men playing low on their made
instruments.
Nero, you scowl and roar,
twitching your tiny ears
in your majesty mane.
Perhaps your tooth aches,
or you remember half-lost savannahs.
Or perhaps you are just an imbecile.

iv.
Evil man.
You are miserable.
You lack power, your only weapon
is your hate.
You push me to the very limit.
These bars are stronger
than the children watching.
Like a doll, or a bird dropping from the sky,
I crush you.
I throttle and gore.
My tusk slices your hide.
Your ingratitude.

v.
I cry no crocodile tears, John Taylor
(for now I know names,
as sure as I know scents).
I have seen the future
and the past, and ghosts, too.
I saw my own ghost
stab a man's heart with a spear.
I stood in wooden fear.
I shook like a giant.
I mourned, wishing I could tell time.
Now I reach out to you,
who only treated me with kindness.

vi.
It's over, in a rattle of chains,
a softening din.
I'm pierced like St. Sebastian.

SUITE ON JULIA PASTRANA

LETTER FROM FREDERIKE GOSSMANN TO JULIA PASTRANA

My dear Julia, you must leave him.
You have gained my trust with your
gracious hand upon your dark bosom
as I have sung Mendelssohn
to a crowd who would gawk with eyes
or fling if they could see beyond your black veil.
They do not question the improprieties
of your short skirt, your décolletage
constantly bare in the company of—
well, your husband should object,
but we know he is a creeping thing, less
a man than you a woman. In your heart,

you know you must leave him. In Vienna's
salons, galleries, and theaters, you have
lost yourself in the meaning of a world
much more than the tawdry. Your husband,
snake, has no compunction to bleed you
dry for money, to degrade you with lewd
suggestions to your parentage. Your
Spanish is rough, my dear, but you have
the daintiness of Castile in the turn of your ankle.

I foresee terrible things. If you die, do you
expect a quiet grave? You call for death
with resignation, a meek appeal to God,
but at what cost? He will keep your corpse
as long as your fierce look generates
gold, and you will be bandied about as an
antique curiosity for many years, til lost,

you wait in darkness, not quite dead, not
quite in purgatory, your miniature son
a mummy consumed by rats.

As your friend, I implore you.

Lent's Madness

Julia? Who is Julia?
The thing, you mean, my first wife.

> May she forgive me.
> On my knees at the banks of the icy Neva,
> I tear my hair. In my hands
> are fluttering bank notes.
> I cast them to the air.
> *Mein Gott.*

What had I to do with human feeling?
Mastery, in whatever bastard form it took—
Polite society had just forgotten
        it was the bull that coupled
Pasiphae, the swan that gave Leda the golden egg.
My first wife, poor fool, could not
even manage that.

> Don't haunt me, Julia, your
> successor too human
> to share the stage with your
> mummy. Beneath her beard
> was a statue's face.
> Beneath your hair,
> a woman's body.

JULIA'S TANKA

This, the least of it:
submission, my jaws are prised
open, my poor teeth
examined, for I have none.
No one else got close enough to see.

BABY-FARMER'S EXECUTION

He should have been pleased,
I took his name. Rhoda I was when I
came into this world, forgetting,
sir, what it is to be helpless.

Leslie was adventurous, plainly-spoken.
Him, he was slow; persuading him
to my way of mind took longer
than a whispering witch in a magician's ear,
I mark you.
But he placed the advertisement,
with full heart perhaps since I had by
every means forbidden him from fruit
til he doubted his seed for his drink.

Christian couple, to adopt a baby,
for a reasonable fee. Pure charity
is suspect.

Perhaps my heart deceived me, at first,
sir, and I answered the replies faithfully.
I felt nothing, sir, nothing but the physical
weight of a child being given up,
exchanged.

If nothing else, God will see I moved
fast. Moved before I could be
caught and ruined, away from the unwise,
in common law,
a blockhead.

I admit that I did it in cold blood,
smothered another woman's child.
It was as effortless as watching
clouds change, turning bluer
by the moment.

The clocks chimed, left me with a bundle
wrapped in crumpled paper.

I confessed, sir, and felt empty.

SUITE ON JUMBO

AN AMERICAN IN LONDON

My accent is mocked,
       my intentions misread.
I'm blamed for
       wanting that elephant dead.
Punch throttles Americans,
       the Queen makes a fuss.
You'd think they were serious.
       I don't wish to discuss.
Soon stars and stripes will be burning
       in a Punch and Judy show
if they allow the transport
       of ubiquitous Jumbo.
Barnum can have him,
       or he can stay at the gates,
as long as it doesn't
       affect my interest rates.

200

A midnight vigil,
like a silent reinvention
of a crusading crowd,
in London alleys
by gaslight. It could be a wake,
or a march, or an imperial
death. It's mournful,
those glossy streets
keeping children from their beds.
The man in the moon
is watching an elephant
taking the reins of his own charnel cart.

50

DOPPELGANGERS

He lay bleeding in spectacular death.
Already his soul was splitting in two.

The derailed train was streaming.
The drivers' hearts were still in ether.

Jumbo was waiting for a confused vision.
His doppelganger was looking in the mirror.

His skeleton was greased together, worn smooth.
His hide was stretched by taxidermists' skill.

His twins rose above the Earth and stared at each other.
No one else could claim such an afterlife.

His skeleton in a museum dry store.
His flesh burned in one purifying fire.

THE MURDER OF MAMIE STEWART

Shirtsleeves rolled—full knowledge
of the blood, the staining properties—
the stench of cold flesh, buried in
a handkerchief—

overpowered, overpowered—

this cruel ice-pick fear, having committed
this crime. He shrinks from murder.
His wife? A wife. A woman. A flyer.
A floozy. A whore. Now a—pile
of bones. Damnably hard to saw.

Something like the devil creeps.
Done carefully—done, done, like
the irreversible knell of a church peal—
suspicion will be nullified.

Get away, get away, get away
with it—

Could he look across time and space,
see her decaying alone in that Caswell cave,
confident that she would forever
remain there?
Those eyes in 1920, kohl-round
in black, a vamp for whom the name
was too little—reduced to hollows?
The rotting skin giving way to two rings,
a barrette, and a tassel?

When they came for him,
he was already smiling in his grave.

SOBER SUE (AS "SEEN" BY POE)

I had just given up the consolations of the bottle,
there being nothing left in the house to eat.
So little entertainment within and without,
other than the debt-coma cries for payment
and foreclosure; my dear Aunt & little Virginia,
believing me safe, in the pursuit of some coin.

My skin was plastered to the cheap fabric
of my own good, but old, black suit. Saw me,
the wandering moon, going from window to
street in less than a moment, carrying a
book like a Bible in my front pocket. I had

no money, but walking backstage to the wings
of the raven-black dingy little theater,
no one prevented me from taking my place
behind a curtain, watching with disinterest
a minstrel show.

Soon it desisted, a new entertainment pinning
the tired and the desolate in their shabby seats.
Sober Sue, who looked like she had come from a wake;
Sober Sue, they called her; simply dressed,
expressionless, nearly motionless.
A marionette, and some money offered (not a lot!),

to make her laugh and even smile. She was melancholy,
so I felt. We all needed amusement, to distract
us from our empty pockets. They told jokes,
made horrible, silly faces, and still she looked unmoved,

like a corpse. We studied in the gaslight a flicker
of change, a twitch that might be a hidden smile.
They all laughed, roared, dazzled in their
disbelief that she was unconquerable, a cold Matterhorn.

Her eyes, though, screamed, like a prisoner.

NOTES

The Panic Broadcast, 1938

A series of haiku based on a recollection of a husband and wife driving through the California redwoods on the night of Orson Welles' 30 October 1938 broadcast of *War of the Worlds*, described in Howard Koch's *The Panic Broadcast* (New York: Avon, 1970).

The Hitler Baby Photograph

In 1933, a photo began circulating that purported to be of Hitler as a baby; it showed a demonic-looking infant. Some time later, Mrs. Harriet Downs of Ohio recognized it as being a doctored photo of her own (normal) child John. No one knows who tampered with the photo or how they acquired it in the first place.

The FeeJee Mermaid—A Rant

In 1842, P. T. Barnum demonstrated his showman's flair for publicity—not for the first time—by creating a furore over an exhibition of a "mermaid," a specimen that had already had quite an exhibiting history. The specimen's veracity was testified by Dr. J. Griffin, an invented scientist, and the publicity showed engravings of beautiful sea nymphs. The public were shocked and disgusted to find they'd been hoaxed, but that did not prevent them from visiting the exhibition. The specimen is likely to have been the same one exhibited in 1822 in London. Known as Captain Eades' mermaid, William Clift had already discredited it, determining it had the cranium and torso of a female orangutan, with the jaws and teeth of a baboon. It is unlikely this specimen exists today, and it was probably destroyed in the Barnum Museum fire. However, a similar mermaid is in the Enlightenment gallery in the British Museum.

The Case of the Miraculous Bullet
In 1874, Dr. LeGrand Capers published an article in *American Medical Weekly* that described an incident of artificial insemination in a Civil War battlefield. Though the doctor meant it as a joke and submitted anonymously, his name was attached by the editor. It has since become an urban legend. This poem takes the form of a somonka.

The Pig-Faced Ladies
Based on the research from Jan Bondeson's *The Pig-Faced Lady of Manchester Square*, these poems look at the hoax and the reality of Madam Grizel Steevens, daughter of Rev. John Steevens, patroness of Dublin's hospital in the early eighteenth century. It is not known why such an epithet was foisted upon her for, as her portrait plainly pointed out, she was not pig-faced. However, she did suffer from some kind of disease of the eyes, which forced her to wear a veil in public, and she was also shy.

The Silent City
This sonnet refers to an 1889 hoax in which an Alaskan prospector named Dick Willoughby claimed to have captured an unknown city beyond the Muir Glacier in southeastern Alaska in photographic print. It was actually a photograph of Manchester combined with another plate.

Biddenden Cakes
On Easter morning, the village of Biddenden in Kent is the site of the Biddenden Maids' Charity where tea, cheese, and loaves of bread are given to local widows and pensioners. Also, Biddenden cakes are distributed, which are baked in a mold that shows two conjoined female twins. Tradition has it these unnamed maids were born in 1100 (though they are often depicted in Elizabethan attire) and lived around thirty years together as conjoined twins. When one twin died, the

other refused to be separated and died six hours later. In their joint will, they left twenty acres to the church wardens and directed that the rent from these lands were to provide an annual dole for the poor. Bondeson has worked tirelessly to establish whether there is any historical truth to this story and determined that it was just possible that the twins were born around 1100. However, while many of the cake molds show them being conjoined at the shoulder and at the hip, it seems medically likely that an anonymous article in *Gentleman's Magazine* of 1770 was correct in stating that they were joined from the waist to the hips. In that case, they would have been pygopagic twins, who have more or less complete fusion of the perineal structures but separate spinal cords.

DVOŘÁK'S PLAIN

This story, most likely invented, first appeared in *Fate Magazine*. According to the magazine, David Lang was a farmer from Tennessee who in 1880 disappeared into thin air in front of his wife and children. His children later claimed to hear his voice emanating as if "from a great distance."

THE CERNE GIANT

The giant hillside feature of a naked phallic figure in white stone in Cerne Abbas, Dorchester, has been the source of fierce debate. Originally it was thought to be an ancient Saxon/Celtic fertility figure. However, since there is no reference predating the eighteenth century, it is likely to be a local landowner's prank.

IPPOLITA PALEOTTI

As detailed in Paula Findlen's *Possessing Nature: Museums, Collecting, and Scientific Culture in Early Modern Italy*, aristocrat Aldrovandi kept a museum of oddities mainly for visiting scholars to study. All visitors were required to sign in, and among them was the only known *studiosa* or female student of the time.

By the Sign of the Swan in the Strand

According to Bondeson, in 1680, Mary Davies was exhibited by the sign of the Swan (a pub) in the Strand (in what is now central London). In her youth she had had a soreness in her head that continued for twenty years, then ripened to a "wen." Five years later, horns grew from this spot, which hurt during changes in the weather. She shed the first pair of horns after four years; the third set grew to a length of nine inches, but when she slipped and fell they broke off. She was born in 1594 or 1604.

Crachami Remembers

In 1824, Caroline Crachami, the Sicilian Fairy, was demonstrated in London by someone calling himself Dr. Gilligan, who initially said he was her father. She was supposedly nine years old and was a mere 19.5 inches tall. Sir Everard Home—termed bumbling and unscrupulous by Bondeson, an outright fraud by Deborah Cadbury—had her presented to George IV, increasing visitors to almost two hundred people a day. Her real father, Louis Emmanuel Crachami, and mother had arrived in Dublin with their daughter and worked as musicians there. They had been persuaded by Gilligan that he could get more money by exhibiting her himself in London. In June 1824, Caroline died suddenly. Her father and a friend approached the magistrate for advice on how to proceed in reclaiming her dead body. They visited several London anatomists to find out whether the body had been offered for sale. Everard Home sent Crachami to his museum, where the dissection of Caroline's corpse was in such an advanced state that surgeon William Clift had already dismembered the corpse. Home had the skeleton and some of her effects donated to the Hunterian Museum. Caroline's large nose and somewhat microcephalous cranium made her look older, as did her almost adult bodily proportions. There is still medical uncertainty as to her true age and the extent of her condition. Her dental age was noted at just three years at the time of her death.

MUNITO THE MAGNIFICENT

Munito the Magnificent Dog was a performing dog who appeared to be able to read and play dominoes, according to his publicity in the early nineteenth century. Engravings show him looking rather like a large poodle, but Bondeson suggests he was probably a water spaniel x hound. His trainer Castelli was a true Italian eccentric who wore old-fashioned clothes and spoke no English but often walked Munito in Green Park, talking "volubly" as recorded in 1817. Apparently, Castelli and Munito rescued a woman who was drowning herself in a pond in Green Park during one of their saunters. Charles Dickens speculated on some of Castelli's secrets, noting that Castelli marked playing cards with aniseed oil so Munito would smell the correct answer; likewise, he may have broken a toothpick in his pocket to communicate with the dog.

SUITE ON CHUNEE

Chunee (a male Asian elephant) was initially used as a spectacle in theater productions. However, he was not very good on stage and after one disastrous season of pantomime was sold to the Exeter 'Change (a proto-zoo/menagerie near the Strand) in 1812. Chunee, once brought to the menagerie, was taught to do tricks and had a very good memory for people who had seen him before and who he seemed to recognize. Chunee did not like some of his keepers, including Alfred Copps and George Dyer. John Taylor, one of the keepers Chunee liked, was fired due to office politics. He was replaced by Richard Carter. Chunee accidentally killed a German youth, Tietjen, who had been hired to be his keeper. Though he was acquitted during his trial, his increasingly erratic behavior meant the menagerie keepers organized a brutal and protracted culling. His flesh was sold off for cats' meat, and his skeleton was on display until it was destroyed in the Blitz. Historians now think his aggressive behavior was due to symptoms of inflammation of the jaw.

SUITE ON JUMBO

Jumbo was not only an extremely large African elephant, he was the first African elephant to be exhibited in London. He had spent three years in Paris, where he avoided being eaten during the Franco-Prussian War, and then moved to London on exchange. He was supervised by Mr. Abraham Dee Barlett, the superintendent of the London Zoo. Jumbo's keeper was Matthew Scott, with whom he enjoyed an affectionate relationship. At the age of seven Jumbo grew dramatically. (The word "jumbo" was originally used to mean clumsy, or alternatively it derived from "mumbo-jumbo." The Angolan vernacular word for elephant is "jamba.") In 1880 Jumbo was nearly eleven feet tall. Like Chunee before him, Jumbo suffered from bouts of temper, which may have been due to abnormally developed molars. In 1882, P. T. Barnum bought Jumbo, which was allowed because the zoo was strapped for cash. Jumbo was by then beloved of London's children, and *Vanity Fair* started a fund to buy him back. At this time, by association with Barnum, Americans were very unpopular in London. After several failed attempts, Jumbo was moved from the zoo to be shipped to the U.S., his keeper Matthew Scott going with him. To decrease the size of the watching crowds, they decided to perform this move at midnight; nevertheless, they were still followed by a crowd of two hundred. Jumbo had a tragic but spectacular death. In 1885, he was accidentally hit by a train. Scott waited with him until the end and then could not be persuaded to leave the body. After his death, Jumbo's skeleton was mounted and given to the American Museum of Natural History and his hide was given to Tufts University, where it was eventually destroyed in a fire.

ACKNOWLEDGMENTS

"The Great Moon Hoax (1835)" was published in *Handshake* (2010).

"The Silent City" & "Silent Sue (As 'Seen' by Poe)" were published in *Cheval* 4 (Parthian)/Terry Hetherington Award (July 2011).

"In the Household of Charles White" was published in *Cheval* 5 (Parthian)/Terry Hetherington Award (June 2012).

"A Victorian Childhood" & "The Pig-Faced Lady of Blackfriars" were published in *Roundyhouse* 37 (January 2013).

Many thanks to Jan Bondeson, author of *The Pig-Faced Lady of Manchester Square, The Cat Orchestra and the Elephant Butler*, and *A Cabinet of Medical Curiosities*, which inspired poems in this collection, for his email correspondence and help; Sam Alberti at Manchester Museum; and to the Museum of Hoaxes, in both online and print formats.

ABOUT THE AUTHOR

LESLIE GRACE MCMURTRY was born in Albuquerque and has lived in England and Wales. Her poetry has been published in *Roundyhouse*, *Poetry Wales*, and *Borderlines* and anthologies published by the Harwood Art Center and Gomer Press. She was Artist in Residence at Badlands National Park in South Dakota in 2017, and her audio dramas have aired on KUNM in Albuquerque, at the Dylan Thomas Centre in Swansea, and at the Orpheus & Bacchus Festival in Bordeaux. She makes podcasts for Lesser of 2 Weevils and teaches at the University of Salford.

CASA URRACA PRESS

WE ARE A HOME for words that speak to the soul and stimulate thought. We publish daring, eloquent authors of poetry and creative nonfiction. And we offer workshops with our authors and other artists.

Every writer and every publisher has a slant. Ours tilts toward the richness of the high desert, where all are welcome who manage to find their way.

Proudly centered somewhere near Abiquiu, New Mexico.

Visit us at casaurracaltd.com for exquisite editions of our books, and for workshop registration.

Lightning Source UK Ltd.
Milton Keynes UK
UKHW011155151222
413978UK00006B/680

9 781735 151694